Soul's Night Out

Poems by

Nedra Rogers

*Dolores,
Thank you so much
for coming!
Nedra Rogers*

In loving memory
of Ned and Jean Rolfs
and Joe Parish

Contents

Not Me

Tijuana   3
Dog Time   4
Day before Yesterday   6
Spring Break, 2003   7
Fundraiser at Redemption Baptist   9
How to Watch the Footage   10
Spoon Fashion   11
Unpleasant Necessities: A Found Poem   13
Dos Pesos   16
23's Maid   17
Waking to Sirens   18
S. A. D.   19
The Most Depressing Day of the Year   20
Empty Nest   21
Decomposition   22
Soul's Night Out   23
The Taxidermy Convention   24
The Last Day   26

Midway between New York and San Francisco

Under the Moon   31
Pine-Tree People   32

Perishables   33

Letter to Langston   34

Brunch at Wheatfields   35

Postgame Morning   37

Horachek's Field   38

Far From an Ocean   40

Pheasant Season   41

Shoveling Toward Beijing   42

July Afternoon   44

Maria's Lists   45

Morning Rush, Kansas City   47

At the Lawrence Aquatic Center   49

Grandma Brings Avery to Church   50

Homage to October   51

I Buy the Dress

Leaving the Place Clean   55

I Buy the Dress   56

Last Holiday   57

First Morning   58

Grief   59

The Small Dog of My Heart   60

Swimming Again   61

City of Sorrow   62

Central Standard Zone   64

The Closet   65

Aleluya   66

Let Winter Come   67

Trees   68

Sightings   69

Self-Management   70

After the Picnic   71

Eucharist   72

Twenty-four Hours   73

Acknowledgments   74

Not Me

Tijuana

We wonder where they're coming from,
these scores of *vendedores* weaving
through six lanes of traffic with shoulder loads
of blankets as bright as desert sun.

We've been advised to keep our car doors
locked and windows closed at the border,
so we ignore this frenzied merchandising
and try to find an oldies station on the radio.

Our lane crawls slowly to a halt, and the street
venders descend. Looks like the Nebraskan
in front of us has bought *The Last Supper*
in copper. We tune in Donovan.

The couple in a blue suburban barter
for a silver crucifix. Even with the volume up,
"All You Need Is Love" fails to drown the shouts
of advertisement for onyx mothers of Christ.

Who can summon enough song
to silence the marketing of sacred hearts?
A young man peddling rosaries and Coke
is knocking on our hood,

and though we've been advised to avoid
eye contact with anyone who wants
to sell us something at the border,
I've rolled my window down.

Dog Time

Evenings after supper and the news,
the dog slips eagerly into her leash
and walks me through our territory,
past lawn after lawn of perfect grass
and tidy rows of curbside trees
sheltering streets named after presidents.

And every evening after supper
and each televised reshuffling of tragedy—
another outbreak of disease,
an earthquake, ethnic cleansing—
I step from the porch astounded
at our landscape, at how untouched

we are on this particle of planet—
Hawaiian shirts and Birkenstocks,
dumping charcoal on the grill, waving,
plump and aproned, from sundecks
shadowed by garages big enough
to house a dozen refugees.

In the different light of dusk,
the calm of darkening, I loosen
my hold, let the dog decide which way
to turn—right on Washington, left
on Lincoln. I've made my day's worth
of decisions. It's dog time.

I'm an easy walk. I don't yank much
on the leash, for the most part keep
a steady pace. But tonight on the horizon,
the great, gold moon of August rises,
and I have stopped, head cocked, lost
in its alarming opulence.

And if the dog were not hell-bent
on pavement sniffing, I'd keep this stance—
humbled, transfixed, my nose pointed
toward heaven, but it's dog time.
She's off to sniff her way down Jefferson.
I tag along, well-heeled, stupefied.

Day before Yesterday

Douglas County Juvenile Detention Center, September 12, 2001

Dwayne is on suicide watch, not interested in algebra
just now, so I'm working hard at making things
make sense. We've struggled through his daily question,
What's the point? And now we're calculating area.
He understands the formula—length times width—
but when we reach Volume of Rectangular Solids, we hit
a wall. He doesn't understand cubic dimension or how
numbers can have power. When I try to explain, Dwayne
throws up his hands and asks, *What you talkin' 'bout, power?*
Truth is, I don't know what I'm talking about.
I just have the Teacher's Edition.

Not that kind of power, Dwayne, I explain
and draw a picture of four to the first power (four apples)
and four to the second power (sixteen pears), but four
to the third power is too much to draw, and anyway I've lost
him. Desperate for an illustration, I flip back a page
and there, under the heading Enormous Rectangular Solids,

is a picture of the World Trade Center, each tower
with its grand dimensions—base, 209 sq. ft.; height, 1,350 ft.—
an exercise in the calculation of volume. The sky
on page 75 in *Algebra* is clear and blue, and things are
as they were the day before yesterday.
In the background of the photo, Dwayne and I can see
the Hudson. We sit awhile, take in the view
and watch the blue-grey cubic meters
flow uncounted to the sea.

Spring Break, 2003

The papers called for rain and war,
but we'd booked our flight
with *Worry Free Vacations*
before our nation took to color-coding,
and though fellow sun-worshipers—
the patriotic or terrified—
were cancelling their flights
that red-alert Wednesday,
we boarded anyway.

Kansas, from the sky,
looks like a puzzle of Kansas,
a pastoral of interlocking brown and green.
Looks like you could reach down
and take the state apart
and piece it back together
if you wanted to, but I could only
lean against the glass and watch
the heart of our country vanish.

*

There's no avoiding television
beneath the banana tree in the courtyard.
Coming in or going out, we catch a glimpse
of billowing smoke and tanks, of mourners
in the street. The broadcast, beamed by satellite,
reaches the Mayan Hotel in German.
I understand only the wailing.

We move quickly through the courtyard,
my daughter in her shades and cowboy hat,
our flip-flops striking the tile as loud as a party.
The Europeans never seem to leave the set.
When we pass their table with our tanning oil
and towels, the eyes of the Austrian

slap my face. The French glance up
to say hello in Spanish.

*

Aren't we all
in someone else's country?
Can't the Austrian see that my knees ache,
that I drag myself up the stairs?
We came here for sun. I'm not young
anymore. When I was my daughter's age,
I put flowers in the barrel
of a guardsman's gun. Doesn't that
count? I marched on Washington.

Now I clock in and out my life and take
Worry Free Vacations.
My daughter's gone tonight
to a Guatemalan bachelor party.
I walk home from the beach alone,
past golden adobe,
under vine-covered archways.
From the iron courtyard gate
of the Mayan Hotel I hear war
in the first language
my grandfather spoke.

We all say *Buenas noches*
in the courtyard, and the Austrian
asks me who I voted for.
It's three a.m. My daughter
isn't back. I can't sleep and the faucet
drips like guilt. Never mind
that my knees hurt and nothing
seems to help; all I need
from this world is to know
my children are safe.

Fundraiser at Redemption Baptist

Gathered round the cutting board,
aproned soldiers of the cross
chop, slice, dice. The Gulf War
is three days old. We're making soup.

Proceeds will go toward care packages
for our sisters serving there.
The potatoes are boiling. We'll send things
women need: lotion, floss, shampoo.

What they really want, our chairman says,
adding carrots, are tampons.
They will have to manage bleeding
in the trenches, in the tanks.

We will send tampons and Midol too.
The men come in with muddy boots
and news. Scuds are hitting Israel.
We offer chili, chicken noodle, beef stew

and take their money.
Moving among them with coffee, black
and cream, we hear talk of prophecy.
Aren't we living in the last days?

Won't Christ return soon?
We're charging extra for dessert this year.
Pumpkin, cherry, apple pie or cake.
They go upstairs for prayer. We stay

below to scrub and bleach, to disinfect
the cutting board, polish stainless steel,
scour the floor, removing every trace of mud,
and leave the kitchen immaculate.

How to Watch the Footage

Focus on something
other than a face.
If you must observe the empty bowls,
avoid noticing
how large they appear
in the long lines of small hands.

And if you concentrate on flies,
avoid noticing
how nobody bothers
shooing them away.

Let the colors of the camp
distract you. See how the Sudan
glows in the sun—gold
as a pirate's coin.
And the dress of the desolate
is as brilliant as the moon.

Rags of the makeshift tents
are emblazoned with violet. Indigos
dance. Yellows rise from the camp
like holiday balloons.

Focus on fabric dyed
for celebration, on splendid hues
meant for music, intended
for laughing and dancing.

Spoon Fashion

What is there not to love
about a spoon?
It was the second thing, after the breast,
that fed you.

Unlike the fork,
next-of-kin to that four-pronged
tool the devil uses
to stoke the fires of hell,
the spoon, with its graceful,
halo contour, was surely conceived
in Paradise.

Unlike the knife,
cousin of the bayonet and sword,
the spoon represents
nourishment and life.

And if you were to run away
with a utensil,
wouldn't you, like the dish,
prefer the spoon—not merely because
it rhymes with moon

but because it takes your hand
and runs with you
into the night beside the little dog
laughing on the cover
of a storybook marred
by a teething baby.

What is there not to love
about a spoon?
To say the word you have to bring
your lips together. Its sound

is little more than breath—
half kiss, half whisper.

Once *to spoon* entailed
a kiss or a caress.
It's what a suitor hoped
to do when left alone
with a young lady in the parlor
or on porch steps.

So shouldn't *spoon fashion*
never have meant anything
other than the way
a sailor and his lover locked
themselves together
on his last night
in the harbor—

the pose their bodies
slid into as the tide brought
parting closer—warm pair
of spoons packed tightly—
the slender, fragile limbs of one
fitting snugly into the curves
of the other.

*

*In order to make the venture pay,
the slaves were packed
as tightly as Scotch whiskey,
spoon fashion,
the bent knees of one
fitting into the hamstrings
of his neighbor.*

—Malcolm Cowley,
Introduction to *Adventures of an African Slaver*

Unpleasant Necessities: A Found Poem

(from an entry dated March 1827 in A Slaver's Log Book; or, 20 Years' Residence in Africa *by Captain Theophilus Conneau)*

I

A few days before the embarkation,
the head of every male and female
is shaven. Then they are marked.
This is done with a hot pipe
sufficiently heated to blister the skin.

This scorching sign is generally made
on the fleshy part of the arm to adults,
to children on the posterior.

This disgusting duty
is one of those forcible cruelties
which cannot be avoided,
for when death takes place in the passage,
by the mark it is ascertained
whose loss it is,
as every Negro thrown
over the board during the voyage
is registered in the log book.

But in extenuation for this
somewhat brutal act,
let me assure the reader
that it is ever done
as lightly as possible.

II

Once they are alongside,
their clothes are taken off
and they are shipped on board

in perfect nakedness;
this is done without distinction of sex.
The precaution is necessary
to keep them free from vermin.

This also is an unpleasant necessity,
and forcibly attended to
as the females part with reluctance
with the only trifling rag
that covers their Black modesty.
As they are kept in total nudity
the whole voyage, cleanliness
is preserved with little trouble.

III

Slaves are made to say grace before meals
and thanks after,
but if there is not time enough,
the masters of a vessel content themselves
with "Viva la Habana"
and a clapping of hands.

In order to prevent greediness or inequality
in the appropriation of nourishment,
the process is performed
by signals from a monitor,
whose motions indicate
when the Negroes shall dip
and when they shall swallow.

It is the sailor's duty to report
any one of the slaves who refuses to eat,
and if it is found that stubbornness
is the cause of a voluntary abstinence
(Negroes often starve themselves to death),
the cat-o'-nine-tails is applied
till a cure is affected.

Here then is another instance
of those unpleasant necessities resorted to,
but it is only given as medicinal antidote.

This duty of feeding takes place
twice a day, at 10 in the morning
and at 4 in the afternoon.
Water is also given three times a day,
a half pint each time.

Every afternoon,
wind and weather permitting,
they are allowed to sing.
Thrice a week their mouths
are washed with vinegar.

Dos Pesos

At the edge of an ocean, I am riding a white horse.
I would not believe this, but to be so warm,
a horse must be real, which leads me to believe
that anything might be possible
in Playa lo de Marco. That dark-eyed Diego
leaning there against the palm is whispering,
How beautiful is the gringa on the white horse,
and Pablo in the fishing boat drops his net
and turns his brown shoulders away from the sea.

When my hour is up, when my horse gallops off
with another, I don't care. The bare feet of Alejandro
are approaching in the sand. I drift above the ocean
on the white cloud of his song--above the palapas
and the little wet dogs, above the bright umbrellas.
How sweet are words half understood.
Something about a small bird. Something about
a mountain. Something about his heart.

I think I'll let Fernando weave my hair forever,
let Simon squeeze lima on my marlin-on-a-stick.
Berto can serve me piña scooped out and filled
again with papaya and mango, and why not
try *all* the cervesas: Corona, Dos Equis, Pacifico?
Why not become more beautiful
with every swallow, so when I stand

in line outside the public restroom, I realize
that of the dozen gringas in their dozen
pairs of flip flops, my feet are the most beautiful.
Even Eduardo, vendedor of toilet paper,
who sets up shop outside the restroom door,
notices and beckons. *Un peso,*
he whispers, *un peso for the regular.*
Dos pesos for the soft and scented.

23's Maid

Manuela says his eyes are blue. I've never been that close, but mornings, I see him on the balcony watching the fishing boats go out and drinking Oso Negro, and when the sun is hot and tourists take their drinks to the palapas, I've watched him in the lime grove share a bottle with Old Mario. I can tell by the way Mario waves his arms toward the bay that he is telling his story of the turtles—how thousands of them covered the beach before the film crews came to make *Night of the Iguana*.

Afternoons, he walks along the shore. Lupe says the beach dogs follow him and he never sets foot in the water. She saw him once without sunglasses and swears his eyes are green. I clean Room 23 while he's away, but not really away. A man can leave a room and still be in the room. I see where his head sinks into the pillow, where his hips leave a hollow place in the bed. I pick up the damp towels, lift a few strands of his hair.

Mario says the jungle used to reach as far as this hotel, that bright birds once flew here. I've never seen a turtle on the beach—not even one—but I've imagined them. Last season, Manuela cleaned his room. On the last day, she carried the empty Oso Negro bottles to the balcony and smashed them, one by one, against the stones. She said it was because she blames the Americans for everything we've lost, but I think she was in love with him. To me, he's Number 23, that's all, but I know how he smells. I know his toothpaste and shampoo. I hold the form of his foot when I shake sand from his shoes.

Waking to Sirens

There's solace
in a clock's electronic hum.
The police car and the ambulance
have gone,
and it's not me—
not me on the stretcher,
not my head bobbing
in an icy harbor
under the glare of searchlights.

I'm cozy between jersey sheets,
glad not to be the one
who failed to change the battery
in the smoke alarm.
And someone, somewhere else,
no doubt, was body-slammed tonight
against an asphalt parking lot.
Not me.

S. A. D.

You create your own world,
turn winter to summer
with a dozen full-spectrum bulbs
clamped about your living space.

You make your home a jungle—
humidify, add tropical plants,
hang vines, or, if you want a beach,
haul in sand and seashells.

You jog, practice yoga, activate
those endorphins, and there are pills,
over-the-counter now,
for boosting serotonin levels.

You keep busy, which helps,
join a team, join the choir,
become a workaholic, surf the net,
get a dog to sleep at the foot of your bed.

You can feel pretty good
until you're out someplace, say a coffee shop,
where someone begins playing guitar.
You hunker down in your seat

sipping café au lait and you continue
journaling or moving your bishop
until a chord trips you up and you know
none of this is working.

The Most Depressing Day of the Year

My neighbor's Earth Day banner
is flapping out-of-kilter in the sun. January's lost
her mind. This morning the weatherman
predicted another week of balmy days
and wished us all a happy
Saddest Day of the Year.

The researchers of gloom report
we've reached our lowest ebb today,
the twenty-fourth. It's a matter of
seasonal affective disorder, the after-Christmas blues,
the breaking of our New Year's vows too soon.
In three short weeks we've let ourselves
down, failed at shedding pounds
and taking stairs, at cutting up our credit cards,
leaving the car at home.

My vegetarian, bird-feeding, bicycling,
recycling, rainwater-collecting, compost-heaping
neighbor is outdoors hanging bed sheets on the line.
"Another beautiful day!" I call out, slinking
toward the garage. There's no sense
in bringing up the Big Melt or the polar bears.
We had that conversation yesterday.

She tells me she's already noticed crocuses,
daffodils, and hyacinths in bloom.
"That can't be good," I say. "We're bound
to have a hard freeze soon, aren't we?"
She lifts the last sheet to the line.
 "It's hard to tell. We may as well enjoy it.
There's really nothing we can do."

Empty Nest

Some days their absence hovers
like a phantom, and I can't
seem to shake this feeling

that someone wants me,
that someone is hungry or hurt, or can't
reach the drinking fountain.

At Saturday matinees
or on cereal aisles, wherever children
whimper, plead, or shout *Mom,*

my head spins around
to another mother's child,
or I sense someone waiting.

I fight the urge to rush home,
but my children are grown now
and live far away. It's always

someone else's child who needs
attention now, one of a city full,
each with his craving

for popcorn or Cornpops,
or his splinter, or nightmare, or fear
of the dark, of being left all alone.

Decomposition

It goes unnoticed mostly, but today I'm startled
by my hands. I recognize the shirt, the sleeves,
but I'm alarmed by this topography
of eroded, deep-furrowed flesh, the knuckles
contour-plowed, acreage marred by veins
that snake like dried-up rivers. They can't

be mine. The rest of me is not so parched
and withered, not as bony. How
did this happen? When? Who scattered age
spots on my skin like stars? I might have taken
better care of them. Good grief, this vanity!
I don't have time for looking at my hands,

those dutiful assistants who do my typing,
open mail and dial, steer the car,
wind clocks—domestic help who scrub,
tie garbage bags, and flush—my will's executors,
who sign my name, slide on or slide off
wedding bands, and at my bidding reach for,

touch, cling to, let go. But in the end, my hands
are not my hands—they're merely on loan.
What does it matter if their veins are fat, gray worms?
I can return them when I'm done. I'm afraid
I'll have to forfeit any damage deposit,
though I can't remember making one.

Soul's Night Out

Soul is sick to death of chicken soup.
His cupboard is full: Chicken Soup
for the Bean Baker's Soul,
for the dumpster diver's, the fire walker's,
the lock picker's, the cow tipper's.
"Enough is enough," decides Soul.
"What I want tonight is a margarita.
Yes, or maybe a piña colada." Soul dons
his Hawaiian shirt, grabs his shades,
and heads downtown to La Trinidad.
"Tonight will be the beginning of my new life,"
he thinks. "Enough inspirational, uplifting
sentimentality. All we souls really wanna do
is have fun. I'm going to live a little,
learn to salsa."

Soul is downing his second margarita
when a lovely stranger on the stool beside him
asks, "You any good at pool?"
Soul has never played pool, but God
is still on his side. He parks the cue ball
and sends three stripped balls into pockets.
When he hits a double kiss and triple sidespin
blindfolded, women gather around.
It dawns on him that he could have his pick,
but Soul is dumbfounded. If Body and Mind
were here, they'd know what to do,
but Body's at the gym tonight, and Mind
is working on his dissertation. Soul has never fallen
in love. He's been told there's only one woman
in the universe for him, and he'll know her
when their eyes meet. But the universe
is vast. Soul has his doubts, and anybody,
anything looks pretty good to him right now
next to another tiresome bowl of chicken soup.

The Taxidermy Convention

> *We can do your grandma and put a dog in her lap.* —taxidermy ad

Back to Life Lotion,
Killer Glue, Headlock Hide Paste,

Skull Bleach, Stop-Rot
for hair and epidermis slip.

You can get it all at Boone
and Crockett Taxidermy.

Whitetail toilet-paper hanger,
Elk-antler chandelier, open-mouth

wild-boar manikins. We're artists.
We can make an antelope

look better than he ever did
runnin' through the woods.

We got it all—habitat glue,
artificial rock, PVC cacti, lily pads

with adjustable stems—just pop
'em in your scene. We got

artificial driftwood, rock ledge,
polytranspar water, snow,

acrylic jaw sets. Wayne Cooper's
Flex bird eyes with lids, eye sockets,

$1.59 a pair. We can create
any expression on a face, even give

an animal a spirit nowadays. We got
WASCO Bonded Ear Kits,

fiber ear-liners, for flexible quality
without the mess,

Fin Magic for the big one
that didn't get away.

The Last Day

The end didn't come like a thief in the night,
after all. There had been years of red alerts,
the formal announcement on CNN,
the president's farewell address,
the twenty-four-hour countdown.

It was easiest for those who had always
lived like there was no tomorrow. Liquor sales
reached record highs. No one feared waking
with a hangover. The addicted could finally
quit trying to quit.

Abstinence went out the window, resulting in
a record number of conceptions. There was more
feasting than fasting. Beaches and amusement parks
were crowded. Few visited museums.

Dr. Death took down his sign. Terminal patients
looked around their sinking boat and realized
that all of us were in it. But life went on.

There were lengthy weddings, condensed funerals.
Babies were born. There were no abortions.

Most of us began to live as though
it was our last day. Some took photos
out of habit. People behaved well,
for the most part. Of course there was looting,
but it didn't seem like looting—more like
an End of the World Clearance.

The devout were joyful, and many became
devout that day. Some, believing this was all a dream,
kept on with what they thought was sleeping.

Poets, accustomed to writing things no one
would ever read, kept on writing.

Babies were the luckiest, we all agreed.
They would never have to know how fleeting
life can be. There were the expected
could-have, should-have, would-have thoughts.
Some spent their last hours regretting
what they had or had not done. Nobody said,
"It's never too late."

Midway between
New York and
San Francisco

Under the Moon

of Yellow Leaves Falling,
a ghost buffalo grazes in the shadow
of the white man's totem pole,
a work of art—eight porcelain
toilets, stacked one upon another
outside the City library.

Inside the City Library,
in the cushioned section where the homeless
sleep beneath fluorescent *Moons*
When Tree Limbs Are Broken by Snow,
you can smell the firewater.

From Biography you catch the scent.
From Reference you can hear him breathe.
At the magazine rack you gaze
past the cover of Audubon to see
that his hair is the color of wet ravens,
that it spills like water over his shoulders.

At 8:50, Security nudges him and says,
The library closes in ten minutes. You linger
at New Fiction to see if he will rise,
and when he doesn't, you think you'd like to
lift him from the chair and carry him
out of History, and south on Jackson to the fog
of the wetlands, where the buffalo
that follows you might join his herd
at the Wakarusa.

Pine-Tree People

Let me in your documentary.
Let me point out where the boundaries
of your people lie, show the viewers
how you're bordered on all sides
by sacred mountains.

Let me be the Walapai woman
chanting the creation story
in my great-grandmother's tongue.
Let me know where God lives,
where my people came from.

Let me be the Walapai woman,
daughter of a red stone canyon.
Let my god be called Breath Giver.
Let his home be on a mountain
I know how to get to.

Let someone else be me, the one
without ancestral jewelry
who can't recall a Galway tune,
the one who lost her people's story
between Ellis Island and Topeka.

Perishables

Just off J. C. Nichols Bridge, he stood
through July like a crucifix, arms outstretched,
bearing his sign: Furniture Store Clearing—

Everything Must Go. Week after week, I'd glance
from my air-conditioned car, and wonder
how a man could stand for hours in the raging sun.

Today I find him parading a sign
through the parking lot of *Pac & Save*
and catch sight of his blistered face.

Get some protection from the sun,
a wide-brimmed hat—sunscreen at least,
I blurt out. He grins and hollers back,

Too late. I'd stop to plead,
but it's 100 in the shade. Instead, I turn
and wheel my cart of groceries to the car.

All the way home, I can't stop
picturing his face and imagining myself
going back—to bring iced tea, at least,

maybe a baseball cap. But I have to get
the ice cream put away—the yogurt,
frozen pie, the milk and eggs.

Letter to Langston

> *(Langston Hughes lived with his grandmother, Mary Langston,
> in Lawrence, Kansas from 1902-1915.)*

I'm doing my homework, Langston: *Collected Poems*,
autobiographies, and when evenings cool,
I take myself on walking tours. Turns out I live
just two blocks from your house on Alabama Street.
I've traced your steps from Grandma Langston's
to the *separate* room at Pinckney School
and the junior high where Miss Lyons assigned you a seat
in the *Jim Crow Row*. The Pattee Theatre,
with its *No Colored Admitted* signs, is long gone,
but The Eldridge Hotel, where you cleaned the brass spittoons,
stands as elegantly as ever on Massachusetts Street.

Poetry, you say, is the *soul entire, squeezed like a lemon
or lime.* You serve us juice of bitter fruit, Langston:
*slime in hotel spittoons, blues as weary as southern rain,
bloodied Birmingham-on-Sunday dresses,
bitter broken boughs of pain, a soldier's cap
lying in the snow, the beauty of Mercedes
in a death house, jungle-lily, charnel rose.*

These summer nights on Lawrence streets, I sense
your shadow at my back. I see you in the front-porch faces,
hear you in blues spilling down from Jazzhaus windows,
in saxophones and Congo drums of street musicians
down on Mass. I wonder at your dream born here
of *a world where wretchedness will hang its head—*
the dream that *knows no frontier or tongue, no class or race.*
Thank you for dreaming Langston Hughes, for words
smooth as silk gloves on my hands,
words rough as pebbles in my shoe.

Brunch at Wheatfields

It was a lovely
day. I had my sun,
sidewalk cafe,
Mocha Valencia,
a lemon scone.
As I was settling in
to that wild, silky
zone, with a hand-dyed
Batik journal and
my favorite pen,
I noticed him.

Toward me
he moved robotic
legs, parched
eyes and plaster
face—a corpse
upright and walking.
He seemed too
young a man
to surface
from oblivion,
a place I've longed
to reach a time
or two myself.

He asked for
cash, for nickels, dimes,
a little change for
coffee. I felt
I owed him something
just for gawking.
Being glad

to not be someone
else can make you
generous. Terror
and joy compelled.

I gave the young
man more than
he was asking.

Postgame Morning

Out early for a paper, I wind my way
through tailgate trash—
trampled Styrofoam and pizza cartons,
party ice still frozen on the grass.
Good day for collecting cans.

This morning, the headline stories:
Fifty Thousand Fill the Stadium.
Pregame Collision. One
fatality. Party bus, a double-decker.

The low November sun's hung
over. In the street, a trail of plastic cups,
crushed acorn shells, somebody's left
glove. Shoes and pumpkins floating
in the campus pond.

On the hill an aged, bent woman drags
a trash bag through the leaves and cleans up
on aluminum. As I pass, she stops her work
to flag me down and ask, *Who won?*

Horachek's Field

You know they had a laugh or two—
those marketers who came up with names
for the subdivisions springing up around here:
Coachlight Meadows, Terrace Glen,
Nottingham Estates, Villas of Southampton.
It's as if developers would like for us to think
we're not in Kansas anymore.

I shouldn't be surprised, I guess,
to see the big yellow Komatsu track-hoe
tear up what used to be Horachek's
soybean field. It's hard to watch
the cedars and the Osage orange trees go.
That hedgerow's been around since
Dust Bowl days. It was good shade.

I used to watch Louie Horachek pitch
hedge apples clear across the pond.
His mother kept a few beneath her sink.
They'll keep the bugs away. I learned
such things, and Louie showed me how
to fish with a cane pole, how to find
arrowheads along Mulberry Creek.

I envied him—all that wild space.
He thought I was the lucky one—not having
to wake at dawn to chase a stubborn milk cow
to the barn. Summer afternoons would find us
in the horse tank listening to KOMA,
and if there was a lightning storm,
we'd spread a blanket down to watch

and fantasize all kinds of things—living
in a fallout shelter, life after the atomic war.

We'd envision UFOs and flying cars,
robots or Triffids taking over, but we never
imagined the Komatsu Yellow Dragon
or that Horachek's field would some day
become Highlands of Kensington.

Far From an Ocean

I'd like to go back to Jewell County one of these days
to see if it's still there—that limestone post
on Highway 36 marking the point midway between
New York and San Francisco.

We were as far from an ocean
as anyone might be, but I could hear the sea
in my mother's songs of ships and harbors
with exotic names—Shanghai, Barcelona.

Sailboats and palms adorned our curtains there,
until the sun bleached them nearly colorless.
I remember coming home from school one afternoon
to find the windows bare, the curtains stretched

across the floor and pinned to pattern pieces.
The fabric, my mother judged, was solid enough
to last a few months more as maternity wear.
She made two smocks, one for laundry days.

I could go back there, next time I get a few days off.
I'd like to hear my mother sing "Shrimp Boats" again
as she hangs out the wash. I'd like to stand beside her
handing up clothespins and watch once more to see

how it's all done—shirts hung upside down and fastened
at the seam, socks clipped at the toe—two or even three
for every pin if we were short. It seemed back then
we had more laundry than the line could hold.

I might drive back, just to look around. I always thought
that highway marker was a tease—enough to make
a person want to hop a train, living *midway between*—
so far from any golden gate, from cities songs were written for.

Pheasant Season

Grandma made us pancakes—stacks
of pancakes, mountains of pancakes.
Before this shot was taken, she called out
from the kitchen, "For God's sake, let her
hold the doll." The crying stopped.
Aunt Maggie lined the children up again
and tried to make them smile.

At Cedar Bluff, the hunting party shot
their limit before noon. In the background,
stand the uncles, tall as trees. Limp pairs
of ring-necked pheasants dangle upside down
in the marksmen's hands. On one knee,
front and center, a young father with a shotgun
strokes Lucky, the golden retriever.

It would be easy to remember only
melting heaps of butter, the extravagance
of syrup— strawberry, blueberry, maple—
and easy to forget the rest—the confines
of the Chevy, the long trip through the prairie—
were it not for the photograph:
the doll, and the way the child was clinging.

Shoveling Toward Beijing

Before geography, before
it had occurred to us to ponder
the dimensions of Earth
or wonder who inhabited
its other side,
all we knew of China
was what our mothers
had made clear—
that we could somehow
make things better
for the children starving there
by forcing down our vegetables.

Then came Miss Birdsell's globe,
the pull-down maps,
oceans and archipelagos,
borders and legends.
We learned that north
must always be above and south
below, that one inch
could equal a hundred miles.
And if such things were possible—
if two inches could bridge
the Baltic Sea—why couldn't we dig
through the earth to China?

With spoons and spades
and steadfast hearts
we shoveled toward Beijing.
Single-mindedly we labored
in our backyard craters, ignoring
our mothers as they called us
in for dinner, determined
to reach the children in pigtails
and bamboo hats, who,

we were quite certain, would be
digging through the Chinese soil
to meet us.

July Afternoon

Harvest is done. The Texas crews
and the yellow combines gone.
No boys in Wranglers stealing looks
from trucks with Oklahoma tags
idling outside the Co-op.

The diner is closed. The sun bears
down. No sound but throbbing
notes of doves and a howling dog
the custom cutters left behind.
Not much for us town girls to do—
watch a devil's claw bloom
or try to call an airplane down.

On bicycles we churn the dust
of county roads, scouring the fields
for a landing site, then tramp
a runway through wheat stubble,
and at the signal from our leader,
throw our souls into the ritual—

leaping, waving, shouting in unison,
Come down! Come down!
We plead until a dozen jet trails fade
and, finally done in, let the lone tower
of Bison's granary guide us home.

Maria's Lists

My daughter, Maria, quit the university.
She's 19 and wants to learn
what love is, says she doesn't want
to wake at 50 alone and with regrets.
She's got a job downtown now serving
bagels, mocha, hot tortilla soup.

At 19, I quit school too, wandered
to New York in search of love, but found out
what a bagel was instead and sold them
in the Village. Maria made two lists.
The first: *What love is not.* It's long and drags
behind her like a wrecked bridal train.

Maria, we had love so hot it scorched
a generation. Love Ins on every corner.
It was what you made back then
instead of war. It was all you need and free.
Easy coming, easy going, love ins, love outs
and babies named Sunflower, Dylan, Rain.

Maria might be in love. She's not sure,
but she's relentless in getting to the bottom of it.
She questions everyone—wise men, fools.
They offer her the wisdom of regret.
Follow your heart, the coward says in hindsight.
Don't, warns the romantic.

If she asked me, I could tell her that regrets
are not as bad as they're made out to be,
that they come only one at a time
like labor pains with nice breaks in between.
Over the years there are so many, like cracks
in a sidewalk. Who counts them?

Maria is having problems with the other list.
Words that seem a perfect match
for *what love is* turn out to be mistakes erased,
deleted. If she asked me, I'd advise her
to give up the second list. If there were words
for what love is, there would be no poetry.

Morning Rush, Kansas City

In the half-light thousands of us grope for an alarm,
turn on TV and coffeemaker, tune in Channel 9,
where Johnny up in Skychopper delivers us
from traffic congestion. He's checkin' out the interstate.
It's problem-free and lookin' great. The usual stuff
on Santa Fe—construction run, volume delay.
Southbound semi jack-knifed on the Coronado Bridge.
Looks like a deer surprised an SUV on Arapahoe Road.

Clear skies are in the forecast, and Johnny says
if he were us, he'd get an early start to avoid
a sunshine slowdown. With any luck the clouds
will hang on another hour or two. Fatality accident
on the Lewis and Clark Viaduct. You can avoid
that tangle if you exit at Mid-Continent Extension.
Commuters on the Oregon Trail Parkway
are whizzin' right along. Looks like a 13-minute
run from Arrowhead to the Downtown Loop.

News anchor Stan breaks in—says Johnny
must have been a wagon scout in a previous life,
riding up to Conestogas to update the trail conditions.
Boulders block Apache Pass. An avalanche at Raton
will stretch your travel time a week or two. Water
risin' on the Big Blue. You'll wanna ford that stream
by sundown. Looks like a hostile tribe surprised a party
three days west of the Colorado. Better abandon
furniture if you decide to take the Mountain Branch.

A million maps and mileage charts, a million
billboards later, we set out—potential victims of
potential accidents, but less afraid. Skychopper's overhead,
and nothin's gonna keep us from our destination—
not water-main break or road construction, not wildlife
or extrication, no twisted metal, no illumination.

Here comes the sun. If we gulp our coffee down and run, we should avoid the worst of windshield glare. I'm taking his advice. I let the cat back in, turn out the lights.

At the Lawrence Aquatic Center

The clouds are not
jet trails today but wispy,
white, believable. The sun
so grand I pardon it
for UV rays, lean back,
bask, drip oil of coconut
on my palm, pamper
the skin on loan
to me. Here

the body kicks off
shoes and lifts
its cover. Pregnant women
in bikinis celebrate
their ninth-month blooming.
Beer-bellied fathers
clutching Coppertone bound
after towheaded toddlers.
And nearly naked
grandmothers who know
by now their bodies

will nicely suffice,
invest in listening. *Look!*
Look at me! Watch this!
The biker grandma
pushes back sunglasses, raises
a tattooed bicep. *Bravo!*
The sleek grandmother peeks
over a novel, waves
her keys, and yells *Good job!*
The plump grandmother drops
her towel, and wading
to her knees, claps wildly,
shouting, *Way to go!*
Way to go!

Grandma Brings Avery to Church

I'm belting out
All Creatures of Our God and King
at Plymouth Congregational,
when Avery starts to suck my cheek.
He bites me with five tiny teeth.
I drop my hymnal and shriek
half-way through the processional.

With one hand Avery grabs my nose
during the offertory hymn,
and as the pastor blesses both the giver
and the gift, with his free hand Avery upsets
the offering plate. We rise to sing
Praise God from Whom All Blessings Flow,
and during the doxology
Avery makes off with fifty cents.

All goes well through the invocation,
but while we're reciting The Lord's Prayer,
Avery proceeds to pull my lower lip,
making my *Give us this day*
sound utterly ridiculous.

Before we form our customary circle
at the end, and sing our *God Be with You
Till We Meet Again*, Avery's shrieking
overrides our rendering
of the invitational, and I finally decide
it best to whisk my grandbaby
away from Plymouth Congregational.

Homage to October

I love the ruckus of October—
walnuts battering my roof,
the boisterous honking in the sky,
wild, blustery wind and gusts
that snatch my skirt and nip
my thigh. I love October's blush,
its scarlet dawn, its ruby dusk.

I love the mess October makes—
the disarray of yards and streets,
the littered acorns, scattered leaves.
I love October rains, the black, wet
bark of trees. I'm mad about
outrageous moons—colossal globes
that dwarf the sun.

I crave October on my tongue—
tart rhubarb, the bite of ginger.
I like temperatures that plunge and soar—
sunburned cheeks and freezing toes,
and pumpkin patches, chubby hands
with carving knives, the lit-up faces
pumpkins wear like fearful masks.

I love October's urgency,
its now or never attitude, its last chance,
carpe-diem mood. Even my shadow
loosens her hair, invites me
to join her, and aren't we a pair—
dancing unbridled through the streets
to the brief, frenzied drum of October?

I Buy the Dress

Leaving the Place Clean

It was the way you swept, José,
that made me want to stay with you—
the soothing, whispered stroke of broom,
your steadiness, the room hushed.

And on the balcony, it was the way
you lowered your head and knelt
to brush away the leaves, and how
you took the hammock down, José.

It took my breath away to see it fall
upon your shoulder, watch you
gather all the color and wrap it
like a tender lover.

It was the way you folded things
and moved the linens shelf to shelf,
the care you took and how
you found a place for everything.

There was no need to sweep
the stairs. You swept them anyway,
the sidewalk too. I half expected you
to sweep your way down the mountain

to the bay. I lingered and wept
when you weren't watching, first because
I didn't want to go, and then because
it moved me, the way you swept.

I Buy the Dress

Because I love
aquamarine. I don't
need it, and I've never
spent so much
on a dress. A luxury.
That's what it is.

Because it's pastel,
perfect for a summer
wedding, should there
be one. That's not
true. I buy the dress
because I want
to look beautiful
for you.

Because I hear
a woman in the mirror
whisper, *Please*. Because
I want to slip
myself into a sea
of blue and green.

Aqua marina, salty
waves breaking against
my knees. Cold foamy
ocean I can't keep
from flowing through my toes.
I buy the dress

because I know
it's what I'll need
to wrap myself in as I watch
your mighty vodka
ocean swallow after
swallow win.

Last Holiday

No sun today. No funny
paper, no slow Sunday conversation
over coffee, just you turning
in your sleep, thin shoulders,
damp sheet, and me beside you
memorizing Easter Sunday.

In the thorn trees, robins
join the choir of Southern Baptists
down the street. Halleluiah,
the liquor stores are closed.
Southern Comfort is locked away
on Easter Sunday.

The Resurrection Pageant
has been canceled due to threat
of rain. No Roman guards,
no Mary's vigil in the park today.
No tomb, no earthquake,
no stone rolled away.

Just you thrashing, me bringing ice,
you cursing life and asking why
I bother. Who can explain how grace
embraces witnesses of suffering—
why breath as foul as this
is all the more priceless?

First Morning

> *When one has lived a long time alone,*
> *one refrains from swatting the fly*
> *and lets him go . . .*
>   —Galway Kinnell

I

On the patio, a bucket of yesterday's rain.
Throngs of June bugs on the water's surface
flounder in harm's way.

I teach the grandbabies to cup their hands,
and, working against time, we scoop them out.
Every last one—the struggling, the still.

The babies find the game such fun,
they beg to toss the bugs back in for the sheer joy
of rescuing. Yesterday, I might have let them.

II

I awoke from the first night of living
a long time alone, already knowing
to lift the June bug and set it carefully down

and to shoo the dog away from the toad.
I awoke the first morning willing
to feed the stray, to stop the car

and carry the turtle across the road—
knowing to water the thistles as well as the grass
and to hold the babies close.

Grief

Incredible, that it remains
a secret, that we
who are schooled daily
by its evidence—
footage of the miner's wife
collapsing at the site,
tears falling on stars
and stripes precisely
folded on a lap—
survive untaught.

Amazing, that empathy
refuses to inform us
of its grasp—
that no imagining
can find the place
where time is measured
by its weight, where
the blessed exist
as detainees in this
inadequate dimension.

Lamentable, that we
must fail the first exam
before we understand the math—
that the remainder of millions
minus one is nothing
but ice left in the freezer,
a cast iron skillet on the stove,
a half-burned incense stick,
a bamboo lamp, perfect white
strands wound in a comb.

The Small Dog of My Heart

Far down the levee, I unleashed her—
past the sheep pens and long fallow fields,
where strollers of the evening wouldn't hear
her yelping or my crying out,

Where are you?

I rattled limbs of cottonwoods
and disassembled clouds.
She raced up and down the slopes
and sniffed her way to the water's edge.

Knowing I'd be missed
when darkness fell, I turned
toward home, and called for her,
but she refused to follow.

My legs took me, out of habit,
to a door. My hand turned a knob.
Feet crossed familiar floors. I took
the broth, the comforters, the pills.

Time heals, I understand,
but summer's gone. The small dog
has not come home, and I can't
bring myself to clap my hands
and shout her name.

Swimming Again

It will do us good,
my body says, changing
into our new suit.

Water heals,
she insists, plunging.
Immersed, we flutter
kick and crawl.

Her limbs propel
us down the lane.
Right stroke, left.
Inhale, exhale.

Beneath us,
on the concrete bottom,
Shadow appears
in her invisible suit,
miming every motion.

I had all but forgotten
this enviable other,
who regrets nothing,
yearns for nothing,
and can't tell after
from before.

City of Sorrow

She believed in the city
built on rock and called it home.
She memorized its roundabouts
and one-way streets,
discovered a jogging trail
sheltered from the wind
and a coffee shop off Goldfield
with windows that allow
full sun on January afternoons.

She knew exactly where to go
for fresh produce, a haircut,
an oil change, the least
expensive gasoline.
In the library, she'd worn
a path to the 811s,
and settled, finally, on a house
of worship offering the most
heartening covenant.

She had heard and half-believed
the rumors of a fault
beneath her city, but how
would it have been possible
to guard against that moment?
How could she have imagined
the magnitude, the aftershocks
that would leave her staring
at her hands, startled to discover

her fingernails have grown?
She is still here. Her books are due.
What will it take to navigate
the city now? What will it take

to recognize the sun again, recite
the prayer? And when she stands
altered before the avocado bin,
how will she bring herself
to touch the fruit?

Central Standard Zone

Here, the gradual
sun dissolves.
Sunflowers cease
their straining.
Shadow and danger
of the day fade
imperceptibly away.
One by dizzying
one, swifts
spiral home.

Colorado won you
in the end—
received your dust
back to her mountains.
The sun that daily
leaves my sky
follows you daily there
and dazzles
at this hour
the white tops
of the Rockies.

Here, the in-between
of dusk.
In the east,
sliver of promise
in a scrap of moon.
In the west,
a momentary sky
between us
blooms fragrant
and bright as a bed
of Spanish needles.

The Closet

Look, she saved the coral sweater.
It shrank and faded in the dryer,
but it flattered her the night
he found her at his table, the night
he asked for her number.

Here, the V-necked tee she wore
because she wanted to seem casual
the first time he drove down to see her,
the evening his bewildered hand
grazed her astonished collarbone.

And still stunning on its hanger,
the sheer muslin. It remembers clinging
to her in the wind that afternoon
his clowning made her hold her sides
and gravitate to earth with him.

And there are yards and yards
of blue because it was his favorite color.
And here the flimsy, floral print she wore
the last time he ever held her.

Fragile as hope, the saffron
summer cotton, the dress she bought
when he was sick. It won't be
worn. The zipper's stuck. It doesn't
fit. But still, it holds the scent
of chamomile and sandalwood.

Aleluya

Easy, the lifting
of hands when mangos drop
blazing in heaps
on the sandy path—
when dogs and children
race through foam
to yellow-booted fathers
bringing the day's catch home.

Easy, the blessing
when the cross is lifted
above the groom and kissed
by the bride. Easy
to laugh when sangria is poured
and rum cakes are passed,
and easy to clap as mariachis
begin and leather boots
stamp and ruffles spin.

Hard, the unbending
after amen—of knees
when hymnals are closed
and pallbearers leave,
after dust has been thrown
the *rosarios* said,
petals swept from the floor,
the chapel door locked.

Hard as dawn cracks
is the waking like stone.
Hard to believe that the word,
even then, can be pried
from the heart, wrenched
from the throat, leached
from the bone.

Let Winter Come

The cold seems right.
Sky wears her white suit,
and I can't see the sun—
cant tell how far
the hours run,
but I don't mind.
Let winter come.

Let children build
peculiar men and coast
down frozen hills.
Let cedars bow
beneath their glistening
new clothes. Let boughs
snap effortlessly. Let
winter come.

Let the lone mailman
leave his footprints
in my snow. Let me be
shut in. I've lost
my place to go.
Let lovers keep each other
warm. Let winter
come.

Trees

I loved them once
for shade and even more
for splendor.
I loved their long fingers
of leaves for giving
voice to the wind.

I stood in awe of them
for courage—
for the way they bore
their autumn loss
and for letting fall
their crystal limbs.

I used to love
the lower branches
best, for swinging on
and leaping from.
I loved them burdened
with peaches and drooping
within my grasp.

Now that I'm noticing
how far apart the earth
is from the sky,
I've come to love
the highest branches
best, to cherish them
for reaching.

Sightings

I thought I saw your hands
across the room this morning
at the Java Brew
lifting *The Daily Sun*.

Those had to be your shoulders
in the crowd gathered
on Boulder Street. And wasn't that
your laughter
in the Bangkok Spoon?

All the newsstands in the city
sell the same news. All extended
forecasts call for more
blues. Horoscope to Sagittarians:
Get on with your life.

I would take that advice,
but your profile won't stop
showing up on quarter moons.
And I recognized your hands
again today in a corner
of Fault Line Café
folding *The Globe*.

Self-Management

If there were a few more of me,
I could let this one cry,
let her stroll down to the willows
to be alone for a while.

And if one of me
insisted upon dreaming,
I could find a dazzling ocean
and leave her at sunset
on a long bamboo pier.

I would locate a convent
for the one with a conscience.
I'd cut off her hair,
abandon her there on her knees
reciting *Hail Mary*
and *Father forgive me*.

And if one of me refused
to give a damn—fine.
I'd buy her a red dress
and drop her off
at a bar downtown.
She could find her own
way home.

And when there were only
two of me left,
we'd pour each other wine.
I'd hand this one a violin,
and we could play
and sing till dawn.

After the Picnic

I washed the mud
from my white dress.
I meant to leave a token stain
but rinsed that away too, by accident.

Last night's lightning brightened
my room for an instant.
Strange, how black a night seems
after brilliance.

Funny, how water
seeps its own way into cloth, seeps
into places you never meant for it to go.
Funny, how you can't stop it
from washing away all the traces.

Eucharist

She understood that plenty becomes
famine, that coming is only the beginning
of going, so she made her heart a granary,
gathering moments and storing them
as though they were barley or rye.

She harvested everything: the vigor
of his step, the tilt of his head, the way
his eyes began to smile before his lips.
At dusk she gleaned the rest: every hollow
of his back, the bold hand, the firm thigh.

And when he was away at sea—
not really at sea, for he'd never even
reached the coast—she had her granary,
and though the season's yield was stolen,
she had grain for the bread she would bless
and break, and eat in remembrance.

Twenty-four Hours

Maybe the place
was not made clear.
Maybe the time.
Somehow morning broke
without you.
Maybe a line
was busy, a network
down, faulty electronics,
or the sky pouring rain—
streets flooded, bridges out.

But the sun rose high
without you.
If not rain,
maybe smoke—a wildfire
blazing out of control,
barricades blocking
the interstate ramps.
Maybe the entire city
burning, freeways
jammed, horns blaring.

Still, evening fell
without you.
If not fire, maybe
war—checkpoints,
blackouts, bridges blown up.
It might have been
the sky was falling, meteorites
crashing, world ending,
night beginning
without you.

Acknowledgements

The author gratefully acknowledges the editors of the following publications, in which versions of the following poems first appeared.

Anthology of New England Writers: "Tijuana"
Byline: "Leaving the Place Clean"
Coal City Review: "Eucharist," "Self-management," "Twenty-four Hours"
Heart: "Horachek's Field" "I Buy the Dress"
I-70 Review: "Last Holiday"
Kansas Voices: "Spoon Fashion" "Perishables"
Lullwater Review: "Dog Time"
Marlboro Review: "Dos Pesos"
Potpourri Magazine: "Under the Moon"
Wavelength: "Soul's Night Out"

My deep gratitude to the Kansas Arts Commission, the Lawrence Arts Center, Raven Bookstore, the Salina Arts and Humanities Commission, the Salina Public Library, the Winfield Arts and Humanities Council, and the University of Kansas for their support of generous grants and awards. Thanks to friends and teachers Kevin Rabas, Denise Low-Weso, Brian Daldorph, Kenneth Irby, Douglas Atkins, and especially to Michael Johnson for going those many extra miles. My gratitude to my supportive family, especially to my ardent cheerleader Beverly and to my daughter-in-law, artist Evelyn Lupo, who designed the book's cover. Thanks to Woodley Press, and finally, my appreciation for the assistance of Pam LeRow and for Gary Lechliter, whose patience, encouragement, and many hours of volunteer labor helped make this book possible.

About the Author

Nedra Rogers lives in Lawrence, Kansas, where she is currently an assistant to teachers at Southwest Junior High. She recently received her MFA in creative writing at the University of Kansas. Though she was born and raised in Kansas, she has lived on both the Atlantic and Pacific coasts. Her happiest hours are those spent outdoors with her nine grandchildren, the oldest of whom is five. This is her first book.

Photograph by Billie David